Muscle Construction Cookbook: Healthy, Hearty and Heavenly Recipes That Will Help You Look like Schwarzenegger

All rights Reserved. No part of this publication or the information in it may be quoted from or reproduced in any form by means such as printing, scanning, photocopying or otherwise without prior written permission of the copyright holder.

Disclaimer and Terms of Use: Effort has been made to ensure that the information in this book is accurate and complete, however, the author and the publisher do not warrant the accuracy of the information, text and graphics contained within the book due to the rapidly changing nature of science, research, known and unknown facts and internet. The Author and the publisher do not hold any responsibility for errors, omissions or contrary interpretation of the subject matter herein. This book is presented solely for motivational and informational purposes only.

Table of Contents

Protein Breakfasts 6
    Quinoa Pancakes 7
    Protein Egg Breakfast 8
    Peanut butter and Berries 9
    Protein Bowl 10
    Stovetop Granola 11
Lunch 12
    Spinach Meatballs 13
    Spinach Tomato Chicken 14
    Mustard Asparagus and Salmon 15
    Protein Bar Sundae 16
    Protein Smoothie 17
    Salmon Steak 18
    Protein Chicken 19
    Fish Salad 20
    Real Mans steak 21
    Curry 22
    Chicken Tacos 23
    Thai Steak 24
Muscle Building Smoothies 25
    Pink Muscle Powder 26
    Protein PB&J 27
    Black Woods Smoothie 28
    Berry Cobbler 29
    Banana Oat Smoothie 30
    Grape Protein Smoothie Smoothie 31

Ginger Smoothie 32

Protein Breakfasts

Quinoa Pancakes

Ingredients:
- ½ C whole wheat flour
- 2 tsp baking powder
- 1 T coconut sugar
- 2 ½ C cooked quinoas
- ¾ C Greek yogurt
- 2 eggs
- 1 C milk
- 1 tsp sunflower ply
- 4 bananas, chopped

Directions:

I. Add everything in a medium size bowl and whisk until you have pancake batter
II. Use a little of the sunflower oil to coat your skillet for pancakes
III. Spoon small cups of batter onto skillet and cook on both sides

Protein Egg Breakfast

Ingredients:
- 4 eggs
- 1 tsp lemon juice
- 2 sliced tomatoes
- Romaine lettuce
- Whole whet toast
- Salt and pepper to taste

Directions:

I. Splash a little water in your pan, and with your lemon juice and a little salt to taste and bring to a slight boil, or simmer
II. Add egg into a bowl, than slide into your skillet, then the rest
III. Simmer and cook eggs for about 3-5 minutes
IV. Serve eggs underneath lettuce, and tomato served on toast

Peanut butter and Berries

Ingredients:
- 4 T sugar free peanut butter
- 1 C mixed berries
- 4 slices whole grain English muffin

Directions:

I. Toast your English muffin
II. Add peanut butter to English muffin and top with berries

Protein Bowl

Ingredients:
- 2 C Kale
- 1 frozen banana
- 1 T coconut sugar
- ½ C yogurt
- 1 T cashew butter
- 1 tsp vanilla
- ½ C coconut water
- 2 T flax seeds
- 1 tsp greens powder
- Fresh fruit for toppings

Directions:

I. Add everything into blender and puree
II. Pour power protein bowl into a bowl and top with sliced fruit to garnish

Stovetop Granola

Ingredients:
- ½ C almonds
- 2 T coconut butter
- 1 C oats
- 3 /2 T honey
- 1/8 tsp salt

Directions:

I. In a skillet heat your oats and nuts and toast for 3-5 minutes stirring the entire time
II. Add your butter and mix well. Ensure the oats are well coated, stirring
III. Add honey and stir, as a garnish
IV. Let cool before serving

Lunch

Spinach Meatballs

Ingredients:
- 1 lbs. lean ground beef
- ½ C raw spinach
- ¼ C diced red onion
- 1 T mince garlic
- ½ T cumin

Pasta
- 2 oz. wheat spinach pasta
- 1/8 C marinara
- Cherry tomatoes
- 1 T fat free parmesan cheese

Directions:
I. Preheat oven to 400 degrees
II. And in a skillet sauté your onions
III. Mic everything else together for the meatballs and form round spinach balls
IV. Add meatballs to a baking sheet and bake for 10-15 minutes
V. Make your sauce while waiting for the meatballs.
VI. Stir everything together and serve

Spinach Tomato Chicken

Ingredients:
- 6 oz. chicken breast
- ½ C raw spinach
- Roma tomatoes
- 2 T feta cheese
- ½ C brown rice

Directions:

I. Preheat your oven to 375 degrees, and prepare your baking dish
II. Slice the chicken breast to allow stuffing
III. Season your chicken per your desired taste
IV. Open chicken breast at slit and stuff with everything
V. Bake for 16-20 minutes or until chicken is cooked
VI. Prepare your brown rice and serve and garnish with sautéed onions and garlic for flavor

Mustard Asparagus and Salmon

Ingredients:
- 1 T Dijon mustard
- ½ T EVOO
- 1 T minced garlic
- Lemon juice
- 1 ½ C grilled asparagus

Directions:

I. Preheat oven to 400 degrees
II. In a mixing bowl whisk your juices and garlic, and mustard
III. Pour this over your thawed or fresh salmon, let marinade in fridge for about an hour
IV. Bake Salon for about 10-15 minutes
V. Prepare your asparagus, chop stems, and sauté over heat on skillet with the EVOO
VI. Serve salmon with lemon wedges and asparagus

Protein Bar Sundae

Ingredients:
- Greek yogurt
- ½ Scoop protein powder
- 1 T vanilla
- ½ lean gold bar
- 1 banana

Directions:

I. Add the bar to freezer while preparing
II. Mix your other ingredients until smooth, and let sit in bowl for a few hours
III. Slice banana and add into a bowl
IV. Blend the Gold bar
V. Remove hour ice cream and scoop into bowl with sliced banana
VI. Sprinkle Protein bar over ice cream and serve

Protein Smoothie

Ingredients:
- 1 S Protein powder
- 1 C chopped kale
- ½ avocado
- 1/3 banana
- ¼ C pineapple
- Strawberries
- Wheatgrass
- ¼ C coconut water
- Ice
- ¼ C oatmeal
- ½ celery

Directions:

I. Add everything into blender until smooth

Salmon Steak

Ingredients:
- Salmon Fillet
- Asparagus
- Broccoli
- 1 C quinoa, cooked
- 2-3 T Greek yogurt
- Capers, to taste
- Lemon juice

Directions:

I. Cook salmon on each side and add to your plate
II. Steam vegetables and serve with other sides

Protein Chicken

Ingredients:
I. 1-2 chicken breast
II. 2 tsp spices
III. 1 C brown rice
IV. Steamed broccoli

Directions:
I. Add water to your saucepan, and boil
II. Add chicken and boil cooking the chicken
III. Take off heat, but leave the chicken in water for another 5-6 minutes
IV. Serve with side dishes

Fish Salad

Ingredients:
- Canned Tuna, in water
- Mixed greens
- Asparagus
- 2-3 Hard eggs
- 1 steamed sweet potato
- 1 T EVOO
- 2 T balsamic vinegar
- Lime juice

Directions:
I. Season the canned tuna
II. Let sit for 5 minutes away from het after cooking
III. Steam asparagus and prepare your salad
IV. Dress with salad dressings

Real Mans steak

Ingredients:
- Steak
- Baby Spinach
- 1 C baked potato
- 1 grilled chopped roam tomato

Directions:

I. Prepare your steak cook for 6-7 minutes, on grill, on each side
II. Remove from heat and keep covered
Grill your tomato
III. Serve

Curry

Ingredients:
- 10 prawn shell, tails attached
- 1 tsp Almond butter
- 1 T minced garlic
- ½ can almond milk
- Baby spinach
- ½ C cooked whole grain rice
- Salt and pepper to taste

Directions:
I. Rinse prawns, and season
II. Heat your coconut oil and sauté everything else, but the rice
III. Simmer spawns with seasoning and coconut milk
IV. Serve

Chicken Tacos

Ingredients:
- 1 chicken breast
- 2 T grated cheese
- 1 C shredded romaine
- ½ C chopped tomatoes
- ½ C preferred beans
- ¼ avocado
- 2 T salsa
- Tortillas

Directions:

I. Grill your chicken until cooked and chop with veggies and cheese
II. Heat your tortillas and add salsa and wrap
III. Serve

Thai Steak

Ingredients:
- steak
- Lettuce
- ½ C coriander
- ½ C bean sprouts
- Cherry tomatoes
- ½ Cucumber
- ½ onion, diced
- ½ C cucumbers
- ½ onion, sliced
- Lime juice
- Soy sauce
- 1 tsp chili flakes
- Hot sauce

Directions:
I. Marinade your steak
II. Cook over medium to high heat on both sides
III. Add veggies and beans to a bowl with lime juice
IV. Slice stem and serve over salad
V. Serve

Muscle Building Smoothies

Pink Muscle Powder

Ingredients:
- 1 ½ C frozen strawberries
- 1 T strawberry preservatives
- 1 C vanilla almond milk
- 2 S whey protein powder

Directions:

I. Add everything into a blender, and blend until smooth

Protein PB&J

Ingredients:
- 1 C frozen strawberries
- Ice
- 2 T peanut butter
- 1 T strawberry Jelly
- ¾ C vanilla almond milk
- 1 S strawberry Whey powder

Directions:

I. Blend and serve

Black Woods Smoothie

Ingredients:
- 1 ½ C cherries
- 1 C spinach leaves
- 1 C chocolate almond milk
- 2 egg whites

Directions:

I. Blend in food processor or blender, until smooth

Berry Cobbler

Ingredients:
- 1 C frozen berries
- Ice
- 1 ¼ C vanilla almond milk
- ¼ C oats
- 2 S protein powder
- 3 T acai powder
- 2 tsp agave

Directions:
I. Add everything to blender and blend until smooth

Banana Oat Smoothie

Ingredients:
- 2 S Fuel 6 vanilla protein powder
- 2 T rolled oats
- 2 bananas, sliced
- C almond milk
- ½ C water
- 1 tsp honey
- ¼ tsp cinnamon
- Ice

Directions:

I. Add everything into your blender and serve

Grape Protein Smoothie Smoothie

Ingredients:
- 1 tsp Chia Seeds
- 2 S vanilla protein powder
- 1 ½ C seedless grapes
- ½ C blueberries
- 1 tsp flaxseed oil
- ½ C water

Directions:

I. Add everything into the blender, and blend until smooth

Ginger Smoothie

Ingredients:
- 1 ½ C Papaya, cubed
- 1 C ice
- ½ C Greek Yogurt
- 2 tsp ginger
- Lemon juice
- 1 tsp agave nectar

Directions:

I. Add everything into your blender or food processor, and blend until smooth

Printed in Poland
by Amazon Fulfillment
Poland Sp. z o.o., Wrocław